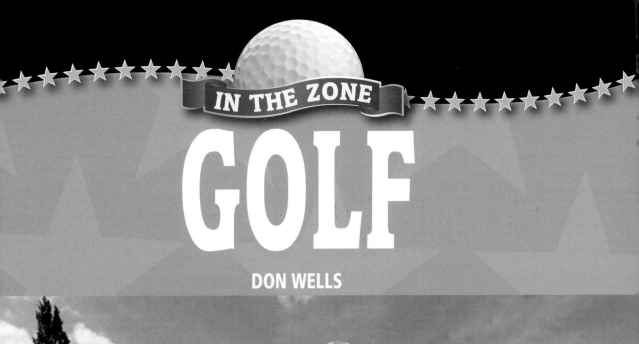

# IN THE ZONE

# GOLF

## DON WELLS

**AV² by Weigl** brings you media enhanced books that support active learning.

AV² provides enriched content that supplements and complements this book. Weigl's AV² books strive to create inspired learning and engage young minds for a total learning experience.

Go to **www.av2books.com**, and enter this book's unique code. You will have access to video, audio, web links, quizzes, a slide show, and activities.

**BOOK CODE**

P 2 6 0 1 9

**Audio**
Listen to sections of the book read aloud.

**Video**
Watch informative video clips

**Web Link**
Find research sites and play interactive games.

**Try This!**
Complete activities and hands-on experiments.

Due to the dynamic nature of the Internet, some of the URLs and activities provided as part of AV² by Weigl may have changed or ceased to exist. AV² by Weigl accepts no responsibility for any such changes. All media enhanced books are regularly monitored to update addresses and sites in a timely manner. Contact AV² by Weigl at 1-866-649-3445 or av2books@weigl.com with any questions, comments, or feedback.

Published by AV² by Weigl
350 5th Avenue, 59th Floor
New York, NY 10118
Website: www.av2books.com   www.weigl.com

Library of Congress Cataloging-in-Publication Data

Wells, Donald.
 Golf : in the zone / Don Wells.
     p. cm.
 Includes index.
 ISBN 978-1-60596-898-8 (hard cover : alk. paper) -- ISBN 978-1-60596-899-5 (soft cover : alk. paper) --
 ISBN 978-1-60596-900-8 (e-book)
 1.  Golf--Juvenile literature.  I. Title.
 GV968.W55 2011
 796.352--dc22
                                2009050123

Printed in the United States in North Mankato, Minnesota
1 2 3 4 5 6 7 8 9  14 13 12 11 10

052010
WEP264000

**PROJECT COORDINATOR**  Heather C. Hudak    **DESIGN**  Terry Paulhus

# CONTENTS

Though the basics of golf remain the same, there have been many improvements in equipment technology and course design

Golf is a game played on a large, outdoor field called a course. A course can have nine or eighteen holes. Players use a club to hit a small ball into each hole. The goal of the game is to use as few strokes, or hits, as possible to sink the ball into the hole. Players finish the game when they have sunk the ball into all the holes on the course.

■ More than 26 million Americans play golf at least once a year.

The game of golf began in the Scottish Kingdom of Fife in the 1300s or 1400s. Players hit a pebble around a grassy course that had sand **dunes**, rabbit holes, and animal trails. The Gentlemen Golfers of Leith was the first **golf club**. It formed in 1744 for a golf **competition**. First prize was a silver golf club.

St. Andrews golf club in Scotland is considered the birthplace of modern golf. The club created rules and **promoted** golf as a proper sport. Golf was first played at St. Andrews in 1552. The St. Andrews Society of Golfers formed in 1754. This golf club held a tournament each year. The first women's golf club formed at St. Andrews in 1895.

In the early 1800s, people made golf clubs by hand. They were too costly for most people to buy. Soon, factories began making golf equipment. Factories could make the equipment quickly. It was less costly to buy. More people began playing golf. Golf is now played in almost every country in the world.

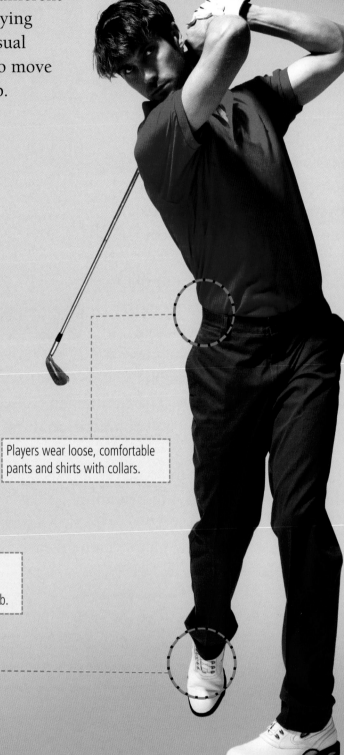

olfers need special equipment to play the game. They wear different types of clothing while playing golf. Most players wear casual shirts and pants that allow them to move freely when swinging the golf club.

■ Golfers use scorecards to keep track of the number of times they hit the ball.

Players wear loose, comfortable pants and shirts with collars.

Some players wear shoes with spikes. Spikes stop players from slipping when they swing the club.

■ The golf bag is used to carry equipment, such as golf clubs and golf balls.

A player needs golf clubs and a golf ball to play the game. There are three types of clubs. They are woods, irons, and putters. Woods are the longest clubs. They have a large head and are used to hit the ball hundreds of yards down the course.

There are many different irons. Irons with a low number, such as a three iron, are used to hit the ball long distances. High number irons, such as the nine iron, are used to hit the ball short distances. Players use these irons when the ball is near the **green**. Players use putters on the green to hit the ball a short distance into the hole.

■ A golf ball can weigh no more than 1.62 ounces (45.93 grams) and can have a diameter of no less than 1.68 inches (42.67 millimeters).

The first golf balls were made of wood. In the 1600s, players began using feather balls. They were popular. Today, golfers can choose from two types of golf balls. One type is made of a solid **core**. The core is wound with rubber and covered with balata. Balata is a soft material. Players can make the balata golf ball spin on the green and move to the left or right.

■ Golfers only need to wear one glove. They wear it on their top hand. The glove is worn to reduce pressure on their grip, which helps them increase their power and control.

The other type of golf ball has a solid core covered by surlyn. Surlyn is a strong material that does not nick or cut. Many players do not use surlyn-covered balls because they are more difficult to make spin or move to the left or right.

G olf courses are divided into sections called holes. Most 18-hole courses are about 6,500 to 7,000 yards (5,900 to 6,400 meters) long. Each hole has a starting point known as a **tee**.

The golfer hits the ball off the tee, toward the hole. The hole is marked by a flag. It shows players where to aim the ball. A metal or plastic cup is inside the hole. The distance between the tee and the hole is between 100 and 691 yards (90 and 632 m).

When players hit the ball off the tee, they aim for an area of short grass called the fairway. On either side of the fairway is an area with long grass, bushes, or trees called the rough. It is difficult to hit the ball long distances in the rough.

■ There are more than 16,000 golf courses in the United States.

Golf courses also have hazards. Ditches and **bunkers** are hazards. Hazards are sand traps, or low areas filled with sand. Water hazards are streams, creeks, ponds, and lakes. An area of very short grass around the cup is called the putting green. It is easier for a player to roll the ball into the cup on this short grass.

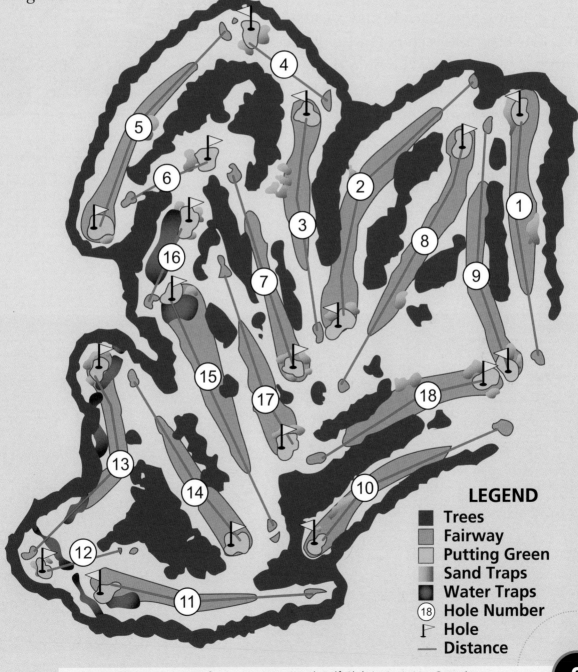

**LEGEND**
- Trees
- Fairway
- Putting Green
- Sand Traps
- Water Traps
- 18 Hole Number
- Hole
- Distance

This is the course layout for Augusta National Golf Club in Augusta, Georgia.

**M**ost golf rules are the same for men and women. During a round, or game, of golf, a player is allowed to carry up to 14 different clubs.

Two to four people usually play a round of golf. Play begins at each hole with a player hitting, or driving, the ball onto the fairway. Players walk or ride in a golf cart to the place where the ball lands.

■ Some people use golf carts to travel between holes. Golfers can store their clubs in the cart while playing the game.

Players must hit the ball from wherever it lands. This is called the lie of the ball. Players may need to hit the ball many times before it reaches the hole. A golfer's score is the total number of strokes used to move the ball from the tee to the cup.

■ Golfers must hit the ball from the exact place where it lands on the course. Sometimes, reaching the ball is difficult.

Each golf course has a par. Par is the average number of strokes used to complete a hole. Par depends on the distance between the tee and the cup. The par scores for each hole add up to par for the entire course.

Par for most 18-hole golf courses is between 70 and 72. Professional golfers score in the 60s and low 70s. The winner of a golf game is the person who used the lowest number of strokes to complete the game.

Some **amateur** golfers can drive the ball more than 200 yards (183 m) from the tee onto the fairway. They can reach the green using fewer than three strokes. This is because the farther they drive the ball, the closer it lands to the hole. Professional golfers can drive the ball much farther than amateurs can.

■ A driving range is an area where golfers can practice hitting balls and try to perfect their swing.

Golfers use special words to describe their scores. Completing a hole using one stroke less than par is called a birdie. Completing a hole using two strokes less than par is called an eagle. A bogey is a score of one more stroke than par. Hitting the ball into the cup with one stroke is called a hole in one. A hole in one is rare.

There are three types of shots used to play each hole. The first shot is called the drive. This is a long shot from the tee. The second shot is called the approach shot. This shot is used to hit the ball onto the green. The third type of shot is the putt. A golfer putts the ball a short distance into the cup to complete the hole.

■ An approach shot is usually much shorter in distance than a drive.

■ Putting requires a large amount of concentration.

Many players use the driver to hit the ball as hard as possible. They believe this will make the ball travel farther. This is not true. To give their ball more distance, they must hit the ball using proper **techniques**.

Not all greens are flat. The ball travels at various speeds on different greens. A good player watches how the dips and slopes on a green affect how the ball travels. Golfers can change the technique they use when hitting the ball on the green.

■ Many golfers spend a great deal of time lining up a putt.

■ Golfers use a variety of clubs for different shots, such as drives and putts.

Golfers must be polite and **courteous** when they play golf. Golf **etiquette** ensures that all players enjoy their round of golf. Here are some rules of golf etiquette. Golf requires concentration. Players should not talk or move around when another player is making a shot.

A player who putts or **chips** the ball near the hole can take his or her next turn immediately. If the golfer waits for his or her next turn, he or she must pick up the ball and mark its position with a coin or **ball-marker**. A ball left near the cup can **distract** other players when they are putting.

■ Golfers waiting to take their turn should stand quietly behind and off to the side of the person taking a shot. Otherwise, they might distract the person taking the shot or get hurt by the swinging club.

Players should not walk through bunkers. Footprints can affect how the ball bounces in the bunker. Players must always rake away their footprints and ball marks as they leave a bunker.

Slower golfers should allow faster golfers to "play through," or take their turns ahead of their group. Players in groups of two or more can begin play on a hole before a golfer playing alone.

On par 4 and 5 holes, players should tee off after each player in the group ahead has taken at least two shots. On par 3 holes, players must wait until the group ahead has moved off the green before teeing off.

■ Players should never stand on the lip of the cup to retrieve their ball. This causes the lip to collapse, or fall in, and can affect other players' putts.

Golfers have been setting records on the course for hundreds of years. They inspire the star players of today.

## Jack Nicklaus

**BIRTH DATE:** January 21, 1940
**HOMETOWN:** Columbus, Ohio

**CAREER FACTS:**
- Nicklaus has won 70 Professional Golf Association (PGA) events in the United States.
- Jack has won 20 major tournaments.
- Nicklaus has won two U.S. Amateur championships, six Masters, four U.S. Opens, five U.S. PGA Championships, and three British Opens.
- Nicklaus has represented the United States in six Ryder Cup tournaments. This tournament is held every two years for professional men's golf teams in the United States and Europe.
- Due to his bear-like stature and golden hair, Nicklaus is known as "the Golden Bear."
- The Castle Pines Golf Club in Castle Rock golf course, along with many others, was designed by Nicklaus.

## Bobby Jones

**BIRTH DATE:** March 17, 1902
**HOMETOWN:** Atlanta, Georgia

**CAREER FACTS:**
- Jones is widely considered to be the greatest amateur golfer of modern times.
- In 1930, Bobby won the British Amateur, the British Open, the U.S. Amateur, and the U.S. Open, making him the only player to win four major championships in the same year.
- Jones won one British Amateur Championship, three British Opens, five U.S. Amateur Championships, and four U.S. Opens.
- The golf course for the Masters was partly designed by Jones. This annual event was first held in 1934, at the Augusta National Golf Club in Georgia. It continues to be held at this course today.

# Patty Berg

**BIRTH DATE:** February 13, 1918
**HOMETOWN:** Minneapolis, Minnesota

**CAREER FACTS:**

- The Associated Press named Berg Female Athlete of the Year in 1938, 1943, and 1955.
- In 1940, Berg became a professional golfer.
- Berg helped found the Ladies Professional Golf Association (LPGA). In 1949, she became its first president. Her term lasted until 1952.
- Berg won the first U.S. Women's Open in 1946.
- During her career, Berg won 57 professional tournaments, including 15 major championships.
- Berg is a member of the LPGA Hall of Fame, the International Women's Sports Hall of Fame, and the University of Minnesota Hall of Fame. The American, Minnesota, and Florida Sports Halls of Fame have also honored her achievements. She is one of only two women in the PGA Golf Hall of Fame.

# Gary Player

**BIRTH DATE:** November 1, 1935
**HOMETOWN:** Johannesburg, South Africa

**CAREER FACTS:**

- Player has won nine major tournaments.
- Having traveled more than 14 million miles between events, Player has been called the world's most traveled athlete.
- Player has won three Masters, one U.S. Open, two U.S. PGA Championships, and three British Opens.
- Player is the only golf player of the twentieth century to win the British Open in three different decades.
- Player is a respected course architect. He has designed more than 300 courses throughout the world.
- Player is known for wearing all-black and has been called "the Black Knight." He owns a company called Black Knight International.
- He has also been nicknamed "Mr. Fitness" and "the International Ambassador of Golf."

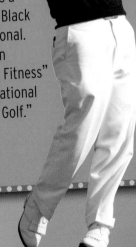

# Superstars of Today

Many people enjoy watching golf. Golf stars are always breaking records and amazing fans.

## Tiger Woods

**BIRTH DATE:** December 30, 1975
**HOMETOWN:** Cypress, California

**CAREER FACTS:**
- Woods is one of the best-known golfers in the world.
- In 2008, he won more than 100 million dollars.
- Woods is the youngest player ever to hold all four professional major championships at the same time.
- Woods has won 71 official PGA tour events.
- Woods has won four Masters, three U.S. Opens, three British Opens, and four U.S. PGA Championships.
- In 2009, Woods ranked as the number one golfer in the world for a record 569 weeks.
- Golf courses began "Tiger-proofing" their courses by making them longer and more difficult. This was so that Woods would not find them as easy to play.

## Lorena Ochoa

**BIRTH DATE:** November 15, 1981
**HOMETOWN:** Guadalajara, Mexico

**CAREER FACTS:**
- Ochoa is the first Mexican, male or female, to be ranked first in the world, and is now considered the greatest Mexican golfer of all time.
- Ochoa is the first woman golfer ever to win more than four million dollars in a single season.
- Ochoa is the second-youngest golfer to qualify for the World Golf Hall of Fame.
- She won the Women's British Open in 2007, and the Kraft Nabisco Championship in 2008.
- Since November 2008, Ochoa has hosted an LPGA event, the Lorena Ochoa Invitational, at the Guadalajara Country Club.

# Phil Mickelson

**BIRTH DATE:** June 16, 1970
**HOMETOWN:** San Diego, California

**CAREER FACTS:**

- Mickelson has won two Masters and one U.S. PGA Championship.
- Until Mickelson won the Masters in 2004, he was the best golfer in the world who had not won a major tournament.
- Mickelson is the second-highest-paid athlete in the world, behind Tiger Woods.
- Mickelson is the only left-handed golfer to win a U.S. Amateur Championship.
- Although Mickelson plays golf left-handed, he does most other things with his right hand.

# Michelle Sung Wie

**BIRTH DATE:** October 11, 1989
**HOMETOWN:** Honolulu, Hawaii

**CAREER FACTS:**

- Wie became the youngest player ever, male or female, to win a United States Golf Association (USGA) adult event in 2003. She won the Women's Amateur Public Links tournament.
- At the age of 13, Wie became the youngest woman ever to make the U.S. Women's Open.
- In 2004, Wie became the youngest female ever to play in a PGA Tour event.
- Wie is the first woman to qualify for a USGA national men's tournament.
- Wie is the first female to win a medal in a U.S. Open qualifying tournament.

olf does not look like it takes a great deal of energy to play. Still, players twist, stretch, and bend many times during a round of golf. To get the most out of golf, players must eat a healthy diet.

Fruits and vegetables provide many of the vitamins needed to remain healthy. Breads, pasta, and rice are sources of food energy. Meats have protein for building muscles. Dairy products have calcium, which keeps bones strong. Eating foods from all the food groups every day will keep a golfer's body healthy and in good shape.

■ Golfers need to drink plenty of water to replace what their body loses through sweat.

■ Most Americans should eat seven servings of fruits and vegetables every day.

Strong, **flexible** muscles are important for playing golf. Training the right muscles a few times every week makes playing golf more fun and prevents injuries. Stretching keeps muscles flexible. It is best to stretch during and after a **warmup**.

Golfers need strong back muscles. A simple weight-training program strengthens back muscles. Many players feel strong back muscles help them hit the ball longer distances. Strong back muscles also help players avoid back injuries.

■ Some golfers stretch during games to keep their muscles flexible.

**Test your knowledge of this sport by trying to answer these golf brain teasers!**

**1** Where is the birthplace of modern golf?

**2** What does a player need to play golf?

**3** What type of course was used when golf was first played?

**4** What is the starting point of a hole called?

**5** Where does a golfer use a putter?

**6** Which muscles are of special importance to golfers?

ANSWERS: 1. St. Andrews, Scotland, is considered the birthplace of modern golf. 2. A player needs a set of golf clubs and a ball to play a round of golf. 3. Players hit a pebble around a grassy course that had sand dunes, rabbit holes, and animal trails. 4. The starting point of a golf hole is called the tee. 5. Golfers use a putter on the green. 6. Most golfers feel that strong back muscles are important.

# Glossary

**amateur:** a person who is not paid to play a game and who may not have much experience

**ball-marker:** a small plastic disk

**bunkers:** obstacles filled with sand

**chips:** shots that raise the ball and are played around the green

**competition:** a contest or game

**core:** the center

**courteous:** respectful of other players and the rules of the game

**distract:** to draw a person's attention away from the task at hand

**dunes:** a mound or ridge of sand

**etiquette:** rules of correct behavior

**flexible:** able to bend

**golf club:** a group of people who play golf on the same course; also refers to the stick used to hit a golf ball

**green:** the area of very short grass around the cup

**promoted:** encouraged growth, development, or popularity

**techniques:** practical ways to perform a particular task or art

**tee:** a peg placed in the ground to hold a golf ball

**warmup:** gentle exercise to get a person's body ready for stretching and game play

# Index

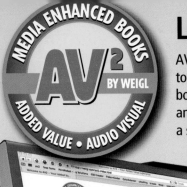

# Log on to www.av2books.com

AV² by Weigl brings you media enhanced books that support active learning. Go to **www.av2books.com**, and enter the special code inside the front cover of this book. You will gain access to enriched and enhanced content that supplements and complements this book. Content includes video, audio, web links, quizzes, a slide show, and activities.

### Audio
Listen to sections of the book read aloud.

### Video
Watch informative video clips.

### Web Link
Find research sites and play interactive games.

### Try This!
Complete activities and hands-on experiments.

# WHAT'S ONLINE?

|  **Try This!** Complete activities and hands-on experiments. |  **Web Link** Find research sites and play interactive games. |  **Video** Watch informative video clips. | **EXTRA FEATURES** |
|---|---|---|---|
| **Pages 6-7** Test your knowledge of golf equipment. | **Pages 4-5** Find out more information about golf's beginnings. | **Pages 4-5** Take a video tour through the history of golf. |  **Audio** Hear introductory a⟩ at the top of every p |
| **Pages 8-9** See if you can find the features on a golf course. | **Pages 8-9** Link to the Augusta National Golf Club website. | **Pages 10-11** Learn more about golf rules and regulations. | **Key Words** Study vocabulary, and play a matching word game. |
| **Pages 12-13** Test your knowledge of golf shots. | **Pages 12-13** Get pointers from professional golfers. | **Pages 14-15** Watch a video about proper behavior on the golf course. | |
| **Pages 16-17** Write a biography about one of the superstars of golf. | **Pages 14-15** Learn about basic golf etiquette. | **Pages 18-19** View an interview with one of today's top golfers. | **Slide Show** View images and captions, and try a writing activity. |
| **Pages 20-21** Play an interactive game. | **Pages 20-21** Find out more about eating well. | | **AV² Quiz** Take this quiz to test your knowledge |
| **Page 22** Test your golf knowledge. | | | |